HOCKEY

A&D Xtreme
BOLD HI-LO NONFICTION

An imprint of Abdo Publishing
abdobooks.com

BRENDAN FLYNN

ABDOBOOKS.COM

Published by Abdo Publishing, a division of ABDO, PO Box 398166, Minneapolis, Minnesota 55439. Copyright © 2023 by Abdo Consulting Group, Inc. International copyrights reserved in all countries. No part of this book may be reproduced in any form without written permission from the publisher. A&D Xtreme™ is a trademark and logo of Abdo Publishing.
102022
012023

THIS BOOK CONTAINS RECYCLED MATERIALS

Design: Series Designer Kelly Doudna, Mighty Media, Inc.
Production: Mighty Media, Inc.
Editor: Liz Salzmann
Cover Photograph: Focus on Sport/Getty Images
Interior Photographs: AP Images, pp. 12–13, 16–17, 18–19, 20–21; CHRIS GARDNER/AP Images, pp. 28–29; Clem Murray/AP Images, pp. 24–25; DENIS PAQUIN/AP Images, pp. 36–37; Graham Hughes/AP Images, pp. 42–43; Grushin/Shutterstock Images, p. 1; Hendrik Seis/Wikimedia Commons, pp. 10–11; Jeangagnon/Wikimedia Commons, pp. 8–9; John Biever/AP Images, pp. 38–39; Kevin Larkin/AP Images, pp. 30–31; KEVORK DJANSEZIAN/AP Images, pp. 34–35; Klara_Steffkova/Shutterstock Images, pp. 4–5; RAY LUSSIER/AP Images, pp. 14–15; RAY STUBBLEBINE/AP Images, pp. 22–23; RICHARD DREW/AP Images, pp. 32–33; Ringo H.W. Chiu/AP Images, pp. 40–41; RON FREHM/AP Images, pp. 26–27; Vaclav Volrab/Shutterstock Images, p. 44; Wikimedia Commons, pp. 6–7, 7
Design Elements: ayagiz/iStockphoto (hexagon texture); huseyintuncer/iStockphoto (turf); LeArchitecto/iStockphoto (lights); Roman Bykhalets/iStockphoto (dots)

LIBRARY OF CONGRESS CONTROL NUMBER: 2022940529

PUBLISHER'S CATALOGING-IN-PUBLICATION DATA
Names: Flynn, Brendan, author.
Title: Hockey / by Brendan Flynn
Description: Minneapolis, Minnesota : Abdo Publishing, 2023 | Series: Xtreme moments in sports | Includes online resources and index.
Identifiers: ISBN 9781532199318 (lib. bdg.) | ISBN 9781098274511 (ebook)
Subjects: LCSH: Hockey--Juvenile literature. | Ice sports--Juvenile literature. | Hockey--History--Juvenile literature. | Sports--History--Juvenile literature.
Classification: DDC 796.962--dc23

TABLE OF CONTENTS

CHAPTER 1

HOCKEY BEGINNINGS

The first organized ice hockey game was in Montreal, Canada, in 1875. The National Hockey League (NHL) was formed in 1917. It included teams from Canada and the United States. Hockey soon spread to other countries. It became an Olympic sport in 1920.

CHAPTER 2
ROCKET'S RECORD
The Montreal Forum was the home of the Canadiens from 1926 to 1996.

In February 1945, Maurice "Rocket" Richard of the Montreal Canadiens scored his forty-fifth goal. This broke the NHL record for most goals in a season. But the season wasn't over. At the time, NHL teams played 50 games per season. No one had ever scored 50 goals in 50 games. Could Richard?

Richard won eight Stanley Cup titles with the Montreal Canadiens.

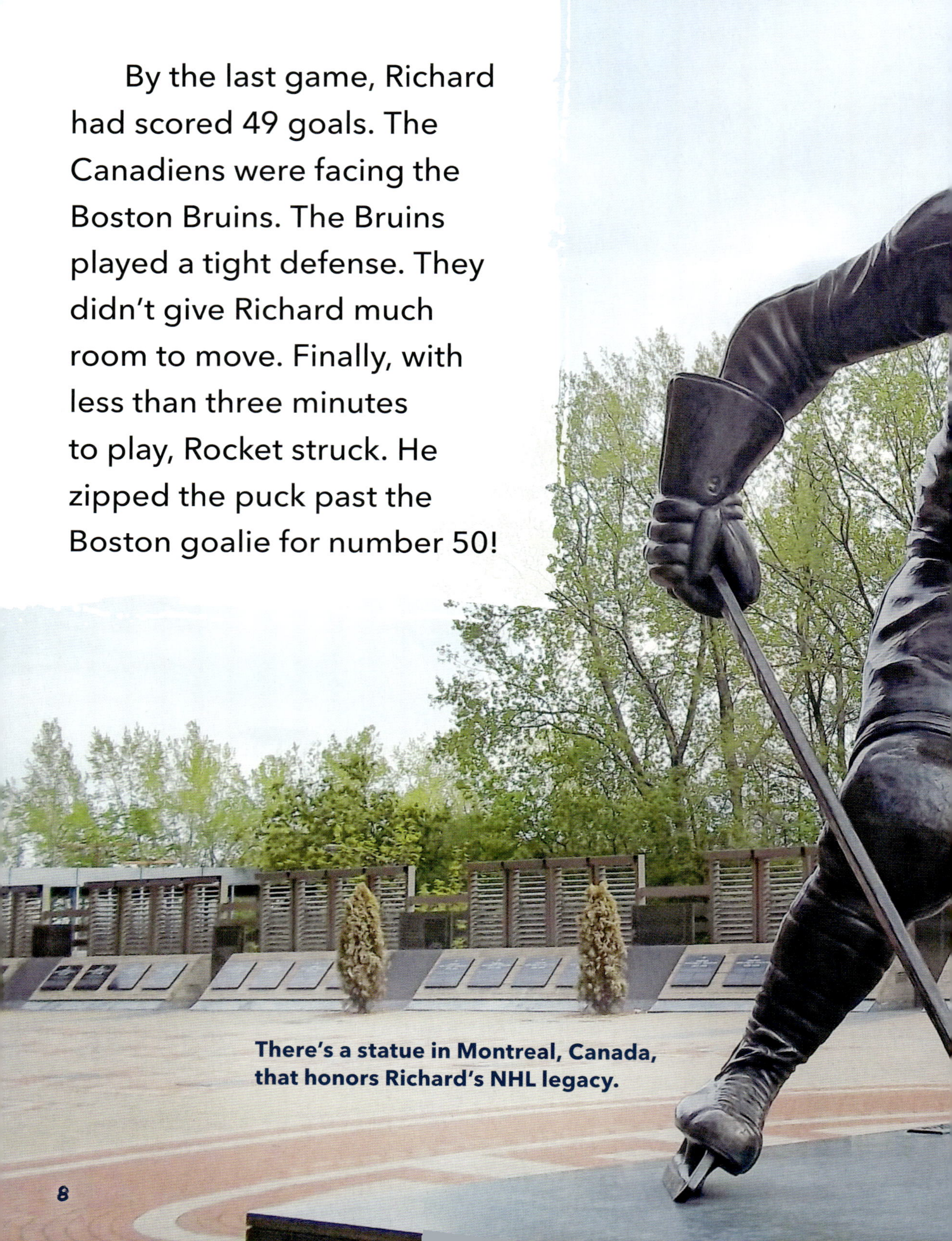

By the last game, Richard had scored 49 goals. The Canadiens were facing the Boston Bruins. The Bruins played a tight defense. They didn't give Richard much room to move. Finally, with less than three minutes to play, Rocket struck. He zipped the puck past the Boston goalie for number 50!

There's a statue in Montreal, Canada, that honors Richard's NHL legacy.

XTREME FACT

The next person to score
50 goals in 50 games was
Mike Bossy. The New York
Islanders star did it in 1981.

CHAPTER 3

ORR SCORES IN OVERTIME

The Boston Bruins are one of the NHL's oldest teams. They won their third Stanley Cup in 1941. But then they had a long, **frustrating** run. Over the next 28 years, the Bruins made it to the playoffs 17 times. But they didn't win the Cup. Fans wondered if the team would ever win it again.

Banners inside Boston's TD Garden stadium show the Bruins' history of Stanley Cup titles.

Orr (*center*) scores a goal during a playoff game against the Chicago Blackhawks in April 1970.

In the spring of 1970, hopes ran high. The Bruins had an exciting team, led by Bobby Orr. The 21-year-old had more **assists** and goals than any other NHL player that year. Orr helped the Bruins get to the Stanley Cup Finals against the St. Louis Blues.

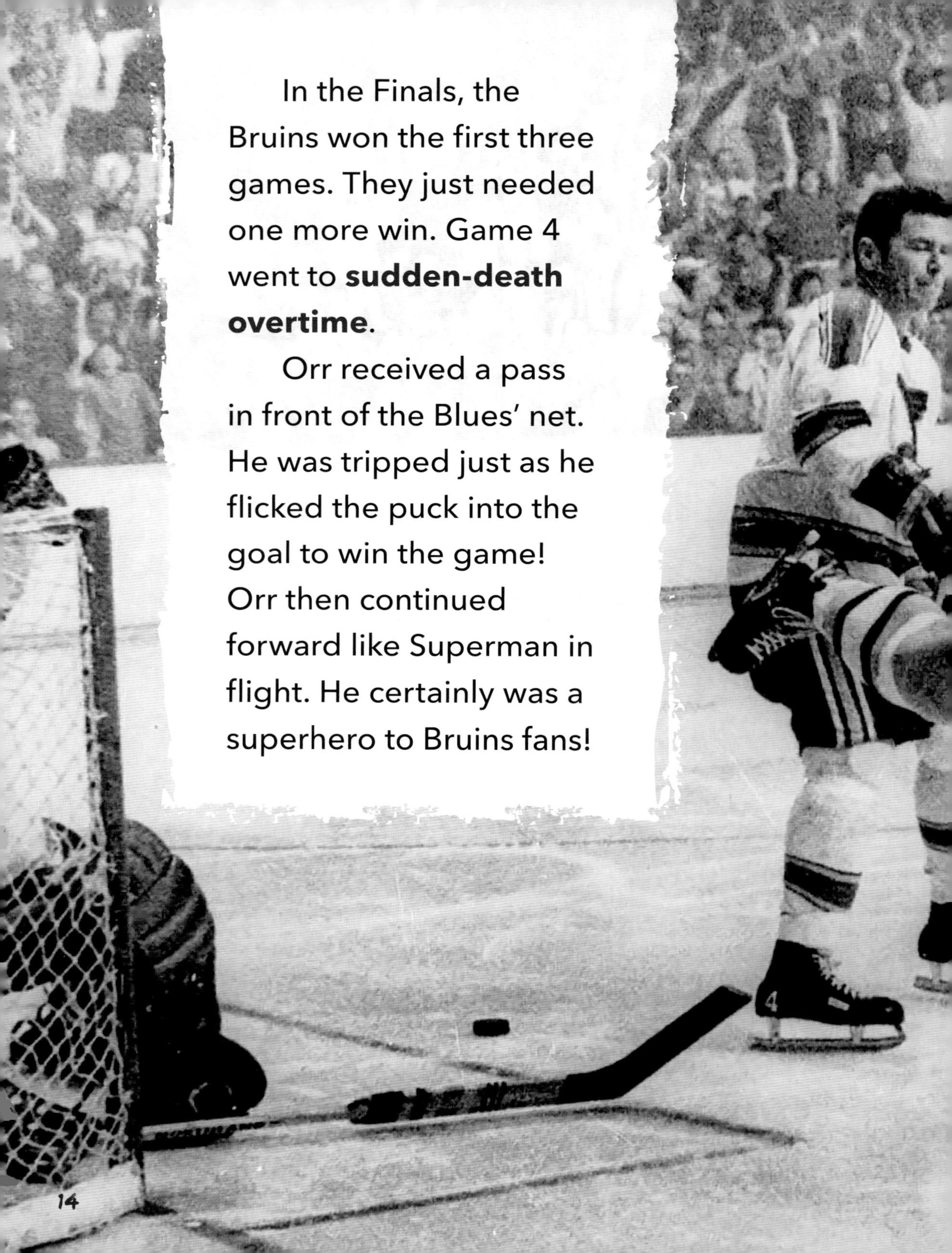

In the Finals, the
Bruins won the first three
games. They just needed
one more win. Game 4
went to **sudden-death
overtime**.

Orr received a pass
in front of the Blues' net.
He was tripped just as he
flicked the puck into the
goal to win the game!
Orr then continued
forward like Superman in
flight. He certainly was a
superhero to Bruins fans!

XTREME FACT

Bobby Orr is the only defenseman to ever lead the NHL in scoring. He did it in 1970 and again in 1975.

CHAPTER 4

MIRACLE ON ICE

The 1980 Winter Olympics were held in Lake Placid, New York. Hockey is one of the most popular Winter Olympics sports. The Soviet Union had the best team in the world. They had won four straight Olympic gold medals. They were expected to win a fifth in Lake Placid.

Team USA shoots the puck past Soviet goalie Vladislav Tretiak in the first period.

US players Mark Johnson (*left*) and Bill Baker (*right*) battle for the puck against Soviet player Vladimir Petrov.

The United States team was very young. Most were college players. A week before the Olympics, they lost to the Soviets 10–3. Few people thought they had a chance to win a medal. But the players believed. Team USA played hard and reached the medal round. There, they faced the Soviets again.

The Americans rose to the challenge. The game was tied 3–3 with 10 minutes left. Mike Eruzione fired a shot past the Soviet goalie. Team USA kept the Soviets from scoring again. Team USA defeated the mighty Soviet Union 4–3! This victory is known as the Miracle on Ice.

XTREME FACT

Team USA still had more work to do after beating the Soviets. Two days later, they beat Finland 4-2 to win the gold medal!

Team USA celebrates their victory over the Soviet Union.

CHAPTER 5

GRETZKY DOES THE IMPOSSIBLE

Gretzky dives after attempting a shot against the New York Rangers in March 1981.

On December 30, 1981, Wayne Gretzky showed the hockey world why he would be called "The Great One." The 20-year-old Edmonton Oiler was already one of the NHL's top players. He skated gracefully. He made clever passes to his teammates. And he scored a lot of goals.

Gretzky (*right*) celebrates scoring a fourth goal in a March 1981 game against the Philadelphia Flyers.

That December night, the Oilers played the Philadelphia Flyers. Gretzky had already scored 45 goals in just 38 games. It seemed likely he would be the first player to score 50 goals in fewer than 50 games. But it wouldn't be possible for him to get the last five in one game. Or would it?

XTREME FACT

Wayne Gretzky finished the 1981–82 season with a single-season record 92 goals. Four years later, he set the record for assists in a season with 163.

Gretzky (*left*) played on four NHL teams between 1978 and 1999. He finished his career with the New York Rangers.

Gretzky scored twice in the first period and once in the second. He scored again early in the third period. Suddenly, his fiftieth goal was within reach. In the final seconds, he got it! Five goals in one game to reach 50 goals in 39 games. With Gretzky, anything seemed possible.

CHAPTER 6

GOAL FOR A GOALIE

Hockey goalies have to do more than guard the net. They also need to skate well and have stick skills. A good goalie can steal the puck from opponents and make passes to teammates. Sometimes, they can even score goals. The first NHL goalie credited with shooting a goal was Philadelphia Flyer Ron Hextall.

Hextall was sometimes called a third defenseman because of his puck-handling skills.

When a goalie scores a goal, it's almost always when the other team has an empty net. An empty net happens near the end of a game. The losing team pulls their goalie and adds an extra **attacker**. They hope this will give them a better chance to score. But it's risky because their own net is left unprotected.

Hextall (*right*) blocks a shot against the New York Rangers in May 1995.

New York Islanders goalie Billy Smith (*center*) is the first goalie credited with a goal. But unlike Hextall, Smith didn't shoot the puck. Instead, an opponent accidentally shot into his own net. Smith got credit because he was the last Islander to touch the puck.

On December 8, 1987, the Flyers were beating the Boston Bruins. The Bruins pulled their goalie, hoping to tie the game. Hextall got control of the puck. He flung it hard down the rink. The puck bounced once and slid into the empty net!

CHAPTER 7

GOING FOR GOLD

Women have been playing hockey as long as men have. But women's hockey didn't become an Olympic sport until 1998. That year, both Canada and the United States had great teams. They had played one another in tournaments many times. Their rivalry was the strongest in the sport.

US player Kathryn King (*right*) takes a shot against Finland's goalie in an early round game at the 1998 Winter Olympics.

Ulion (*center*) hugs teammate Jennifer Schmidgall after scoring during the gold medal match against Canada.

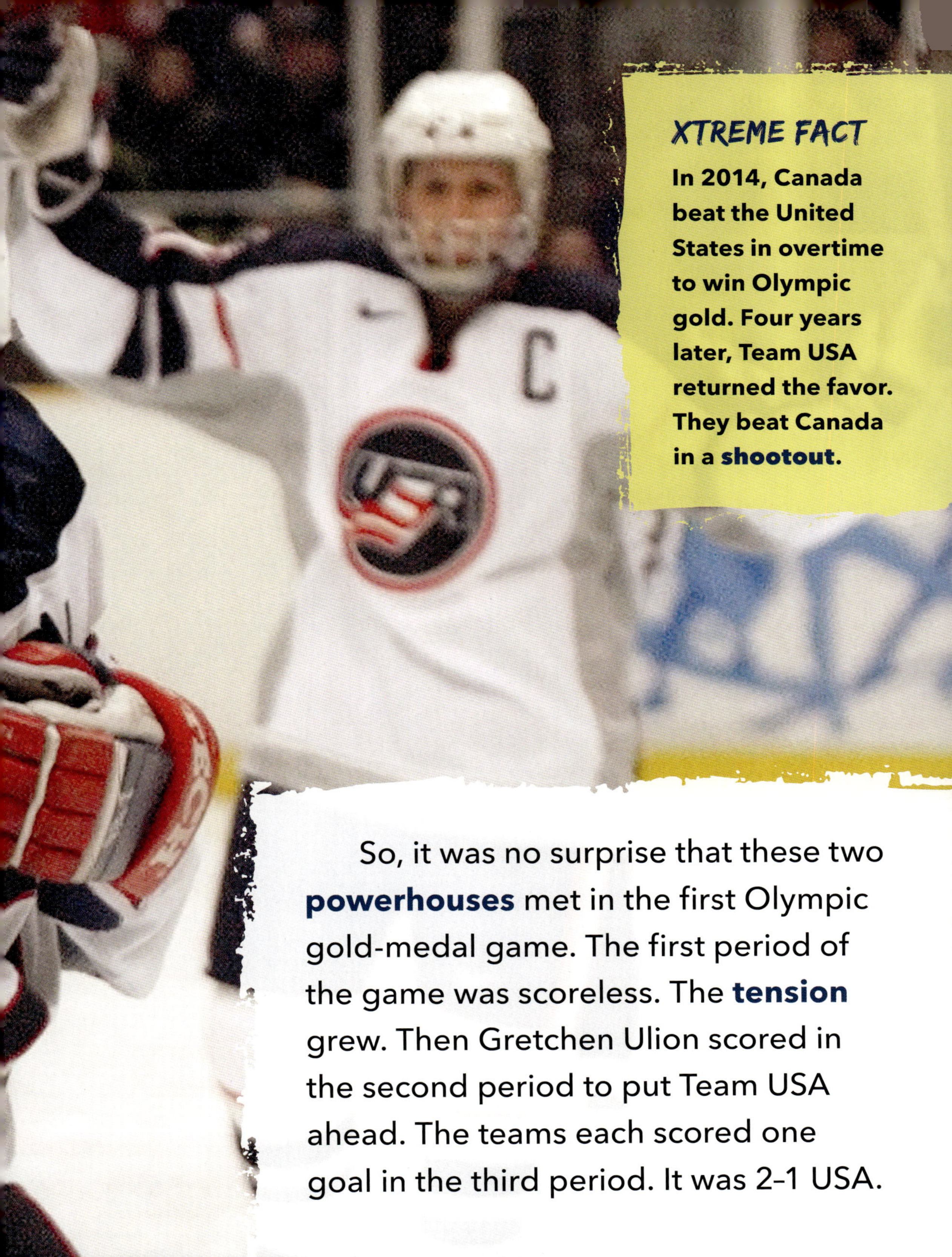

So, it was no surprise that these two **powerhouses** met in the first Olympic gold-medal game. The first period of the game was scoreless. The **tension** grew. Then Gretchen Ulion scored in the second period to put Team USA ahead. The teams each scored one goal in the third period. It was 2–1 USA.

Canada pressed hard to tie the game. They removed their goalie to gain more offense. Then Sandra Whyte scored an empty-net goal for Team USA. This made the score 3–1. Canada was unable to score. Team USA won the first Olympic gold medal in women's hockey!

TRICK SHOT

Trevor Zegras of the Anaheim Ducks is known for his flashy moves on the ice. But the goal he scored on January 27, 2022, will be talked about for years. That day, the Ducks were in Montreal to take on the Canadiens. In the second period, Zegras got control of the puck near the Canadiens' net. He skated behind the net with the puck.

Zegras played college hockey at Boston University. He was selected by the Anaheim Ducks in the 2019 NHL Entry Draft.

7UP

The Canadiens goalie expected Zegras to pass the puck to a teammate in front of the net. Instead, Zegras picked up the puck on the blade of his stick. He carried the puck around the net and tucked it over the goalie's shoulder. The stunned Canadiens could only watch as Zegras and the Ducks celebrated the unexpected goal.

XTREME FACT

On February 7, 1976, Darryl Sittler of the Toronto Maple Leafs made history. He scored six goals and had four **assists** in an 11-4 win over the Boston Bruins. Sittler's 10 points are the most by one player in an NHL game.

CHAPTER 9

THE FUTURE OF HOCKEY

Hockey is one of the most popular sports in the world. Every year, exciting new players become fan favorites. Auston Matthews, Alex Ovechkin, Kirill Kaprizov, Gabbie Hughes, and Sophie Jaques are just a few of the latest superstars to thrill fans and make memories on the ice.

XTREME CHALLENGE

TAKE THE QUIZ BELOW AND
PUT WHAT YOU'VE LEARNED TO THE TEST!

1) How many games did an NHL team play in the regular season in 1945?

2) Who is the only defenseman ever to lead the NHL in scoring?

3) Who scored the winning goal for Team USA against the Soviet Union in 1980?

4) Why is it risky for a team to pull its goalie?

5) Which country is Team USA's biggest rival in women's hockey?

GLOSSARY

assist—in sports, an action of a player that allows a teammate to score a goal.

attacker—in hockey, a player whose main job is to shoot the puck at the goal.

frustrating—causing feelings of anger, annoyance, or disappointment.

powerhouse—a team that is known for strong, aggressive play and that often wins.

shootout—a shooting competition that is used to determine the winner of a game that ends in a tie.

sudden-death overtime—an additional period of play during which the first team to score wins the game.

tension—a feeling of anticipation and excitement.

ONLINE RESOURCES

To learn more about hockey, please visit **abdobooklinks.com** or scan this QR code. These links are routinely monitored and updated to provide the most current information available.

INDEX